WORLD OF
MAMMALS

SKUNKS

By Sophie Lockwood

Content Adviser: Barbara E. Brown, Scientific Associate, Mammal Division, Field Museum of Chicago

THE CHILD'S WORLD®, MANKATO, MINNESOTA

Skunks

Published in the United States of America by The Child's World®
1980 Lookout Drive • Mankato, MN 56003-1705
800-599-READ • www.childsworld.com

Acknowledgements:

The Child's World®: Mary Berendes, Publishing Director

The Creative Spark: Mary Francis, Project Director; Wendy Mead, Editor; Deborah Goodsite, Photo Researcher

The Design Lab: Kathleen Petelinsek, Designer and Production Artist

Photos:

Cover and half title: DLILLC/Corbis; frontispiece and page 4: Ruth Hoyt/Alamy.

Interior: Alamy: 9 (Bruce Coleman Inc.), 5 center left and 21 (Arco Images), 26 (blickwinkel); Dreamstime.com: 5 top right and 14 (Holly Kuchera); The Image Works: 34 (Mary Evans Picture Library); Minden Pictures: 13 (Konrad Wothe), 16 (Claus Meyer); Peter Arnold Inc.: 37 (Matt Meadows); Photolibrary Group: 5 top left and 10; Photo Researchers, Inc.: 5 bottom right and 25 (Anthony Mercieca); Visuals Unlimited: 18 (Dr. Gilbert Twiest), 23 (Joe McDonald), 28 (Tom J. Ulrich), 5 bottom left and 33 (William Weber).

Library of Congress Cataloging-in-Publication Data

Lockwood, Sophie.
  Skunks / by Sophie Lockwood.
      p. cm. — (The World of mammals)
  Includes index.
  ISBN 978-1-59296-929-6 (library bound : alk. paper)
  1. Skunks—Juvenile literature. I. Title. II. Series.
  QL737.C248L63 2008
  599.76'8—dc22   2007022219

TABLE OF CONTENTS

Chapter One

The Year of the Skunk

On the slopes of the San Juan Mountains in Colorado, a young coyote makes a big mistake. The coyote notices a rustle in the underbrush and goes to explore. The animal causing the rustle is a western spotted skunk (*Spilogale gracilis*), a small skunk species that packs a seriously foul stink.

The skunk takes one look at the coyote and begins to stamp its front feet. This coyote has never come across a skunk before and does not recognize this warning signal. The skunk does a handstand, curling its tail over to show its weapon. The coyote seems more than a bit curious and does not leave. The skunk curls its body into a U-shape, takes aim, and fires—a direct hit of revolting-smelling, yellow liquid right in the coyote's face. This stinky spray can blind an animal. Yelping, the coyote runs away as the skunk settles down to munch on a tasty grouse egg.

Did You Know?
Spotted skunks are the smallest skunk species. Males measure 35 to 58 centimeters (13.8 to 22.8 inches) long, and tails add another 10 to 21 centimeters (3.9 to 8.2 inches). Females measure 17 to 47 centimeters (6.7 to 18.5 inches) long, with 8.5- to 20-centimeter (3.5- to 7.9-inch) tails. Males weigh, on average, 700 grams (1.5 pounds) while females weigh about 400 grams (0.9 pounds).

Range of the
Western Spotted Skunk

CANADA

U.S.A.

MEXICO

*Atlantic
Ocean*

Gulf of Mexico

*Pacific
Ocean*

This map shows the western spotted skunk's habitats.

It is September—mating time for spotted skunks. The female wants to find a male to mate with. Spotted skunks sleep during the day and hunt in the early evening and night, so her best chance to find a mate is while hunting. However, the males tend to live lonely lives. The lucky female and a strange male come across each other late one night in a dry riverbed. They mate.

Although she has mated, she is not pregnant. Her eggs have been fertilized, but they will not become **embryos** immediately. Winter is not a good time for having offspring because there is too little food available. The female skunk will hold the fertilized eggs in her body until later, when she will be able to provide food for her babies, called kits. This process is called **delayed implantation.** The embryos do not begin to grow into kits until springtime. This allows the female skunk to mate when males are at their sexual peak but not give birth to young until food is plentiful.

Winter is coming, and the spotted skunk begins to put on weight. Spotted skunks do not really **hibernate** through the winter, but they do slow down and sleep often. Females often bunk together through the cold Colorado winter. This year, a group of females has found a shallow

cave on the side of a rocky cliff for a den.
A haystack, a barn, a drainpipe, or a hollow log would have done as well. Up to

A spotted skunk searches for food in a western forest.

Unlike female spotted skunks, the males spend most of their lives alone.

twenty females huddle together against the cold to sleep for several weeks.

After a long winter, the embryos become active in the female's womb. The kits are born after twenty-eight to thirty-one days. She delivers four healthy young, each weighing about 23 grams (0.8 ounce). Fine black-and-white hair covers the kits in the spot pattern they will wear throughout their lives. By one month old, their eyes will be open. Between seven and eight weeks, the kits are fully weaned from their mother's milk and are rooting around the scrub brush for grasshoppers, mice, roots, berries, and scorpions.

Females become sexually mature at four to five months, and will mate in the fall of the year they are born. Two of the kits are females and will be mothers at about the time they reach a year old.

Skunk kits are armed and ready to fire at less than one month old. A skunk's only protection is its spray, and even young skunks can protect themselves. Their aim is accurate up to about 3 meters (9.8 feet). Even so, many young skunks die from attacks by birds of prey, coyotes, and bobcats.

Chapter Two

Black and White and Lives All Over

A striped skunk (*Mephitis mephitis*) waddles out of the woods in the Adirondack Mountains of New York. When most people think skunk, this is the picture they have in their minds. The striped skunk has two dramatic white stripes, one on each side of the body. The stripes meet on the top of the skunk's head in a cap. The back and the rest of the body are black.

Skunk fur shouts a warning. Many animals have dramatic coloring that warns **predators** that they are dangerous. The danger may be poison, venom or, in the case of skunks, stink. This type of coloring on an animal is called **aposematic.** Skunk fur says, "Stay away, or you'll be sorry."

True skunks come in variations of black-and-white fur. Hooded skunks have white backs and fluffy white tails. Spotted skunks have spots instead of stripes. Hog-nosed

skunks are white on the top half of their bodies and black on the bottom.

Skunk bodies are short and squat, about the size of a pet cat. The largest skunks are striped skunks. They can weigh up to 6.4 kilograms (14 pounds). The smallest skunks—spotted skunks—rarely weigh more than 0.9 kilograms (2 pounds). Hog-nosed and hooded skunks

Even baby skunks, like this young striped skunk, can spray!

average about 2.3 kilograms (5.1 pounds). Tails add length to the body, but very little weight. Most skunks' tails equal 40 to 100 percent of their body length, but they are fluffy and almost featherlike in appearance.

Skunks have short legs with front paws armed with sharp, powerful claws. The claws are useful for digging burrows or rooting around for grubs, worms, and insects underground.

As predators go, skunks cannot move fast enough to actually chase their prey. Their top speed is about 16 kilometers per hour (10 miles per hour), and they cannot run at that pace for very long. Skunks are more

Would you Believe?
Two skunks in the Exmoor Zoo in Devon, England, gave birth to a litter of kits, two of which were albinos. This means that they have all-white fur and pink eyes. Mutations like this might happen once in 20,000 births. In nature, this coloring would be dangerous, as predators would not recognize these animals as skunks.

This curious bear cub might run home with awful-smelling skunk spray on its fur.

likely to stalk a small critter or lie in wait until something tasty comes along. They also will raid the food **caches** of other animals, particularly weasels.

Perhaps because they are so slow, skunks have adapted to eating a wide variety of foods. Most skunks eat great quantities of insects, although not always the same species. Striped skunks prefer bees, while hog-nosed skunks like grubs, and hooded skunks like beetles.

Skunks are **omnivores**—they eat almost anything. Most skunks will eat birds and bird eggs, a range of insects, frogs, crayfish, rodents, lizards, berries, grapes, corn, and other plant matter. Spotted skunks may also eat venomous snakes. Hog-nosed skunks use their long, piglike snouts to uncover creatures living underground. Insect larvae are particularly yummy to hog-nosed skunks.

Most skunks will also eat **carrion.** The rotting corpse of a dead wolf, coyote, bear, or any other animal provides quality protein. Skunk stomachs are able to digest rotting flesh, and skunks will not get sick from it. Skunks also eat garbage. If a dog or a raccoon tips over a garbage can, a skunk will take advantage of the opportunity to get a quick and easy meal.

A skunk's diet tends to change with the seasons because the available foods change. For example, insects and **arachnids**

make up 94 percent of the hog-nosed skunk's diet in spring. During the summer, that drops to under 60 percent, with plant matter (fruits) making up about 30 percent of the food.

Fall sees a decrease in insects and arachnids and an increase in plant matter to nearly 40 percent. As plant food becomes less available during the winter, the hog-nosed skunk increases its insect intake.

Would You Believe?
Once upon a time, perfumers used musk from skunks in making perfume. Yes, the musk is the source of the skunk's horrid odor.

Hog-nosed skunks like to feed on bugs and plants.

Chapter Three

Whew! What a Stink!

Skunks do everything they can to avoid spraying. They stamp their feet and hiss. They raise their tails as a warning and may even snap their teeth, grunt, whine, chirp, and squeal like a pig. If none of those warning signs work, whatever is causing the skunk trouble gets the spray.

Since spraying is a skunk's sole means of defense, why would a skunk *not* want to spray? For one thing, skunks cannot stand the smell themselves. Skunks will not spray other skunks during a fight, nor will they spray near their own dens. Most skunks will not spray unless they have a clear escape route. Trapped in the back of a burrow—particularly its own burrow—a skunk will probably not spray.

Another reason for a skunk to avoid spraying is the limited amount of ammunition. Most skunks only have enough spray to last five or six squirts. It could take ten days to manufacture more. The scent is manufactured and stored in small glands on either side of the **anus.** Each gland has a nipple and muscles to

Did You Know?
The television show *Myth-busters* ran a program testing home remedies for getting rid of skunk odors. They found that a combination of hydrogen peroxide, baking soda, and liquid soap worked better than tomato juice or vinegar.

control the amount and direction of the spray. The spray itself is made up of sulfur-based chemical compounds called **thiols.** The best description of the scent is a combination of rotten eggs, garlic, and burning rubber.

Even young skunks can hit a target from 2 to 3 meters (6.7 to 9.8 feet) away. They are less accurate at distances up to 6 or 7 meters (19.7 to 23 feet). The odor, however,

This photograph shows a young striped skunk preparing to spray a dog that has gotten too close.

is strong enough that even humans, who have a fairly poor sense of smell, can catch the stink up to 1.6 kilometers (1 mile) away.

SKUNK LIFESTYLES

Considering the dangers of being sprayed, it might seem that skunks would have no predators interested in them. Spraying does not protect skunks from birds of prey, such as red-tailed hawks, great horned owls, golden eagles, and bald eagles. These animals swoop down from the sky and pluck their prey before the skunk has a chance to spray. The skunk's greatest enemy is the great horned owl, because great horned owls have almost no sense of smell. On occasion, a coyote or a dog gets lucky and captures a skunk before it can spray.

Despite having a small number of predators for an animal of its size, skunks have very short life spans. The average skunk dies before reaching three years old. The greatest cause of untimely skunk deaths is being struck by cars. Skunks cannot move quickly enough to get out of the way, and many drivers react too slowly to swerve away from a skunk in the road. The result is a dead skunk and a car that stinks for weeks, no matter how many times it is washed.

HOME SWEET HOME

Skunks are fully capable of digging their own dens, but most prefer to move in on someone else's. Skunks will take over empty wood rat or porcupine burrows. They will even allow the original owners to share the burrows with them. A snug burrow is important, and many skunks line their burrows with leaves, ferns, or other matter to make them comfortable.

A good den does not have to be a burrow or even located in the wild. Skunks are highly adaptable. They may come across a hollow log or a hole in a tree and use that space for a burrow. Brush piles, woodpiles, and haystacks provide excellent shelter, as do barns, attics, and crawl spaces under houses. Skunks also live under rocky ledges, in caves, and in open drainpipes. A garbage dump can become an ideal home for a skunk—housing and food combined.

Would You Believe?

A California skunk went to sleep in a large rubber pipe in Torrance, California. The pipe was loaded onto a truck. The next thing the skunk knew it was in Toronto, Canada. Returning the skunk to California became a serious problem. Airlines do not wish to carry a skunk, and Canada could not legally release a foreign species into the wild. Besides, Canadian skunks are larger than the California skunk and would probably have killed the foreigner eventually. The skunk was taken home to California by truck—the same way it traveled to Canada.

One time a true den is important is when a female skunk births a litter of kits. Most skunk litters have two to six kits. The kits are almost defenseless, and the mother needs a safe place to stash them for the first month or so. The male was only present for mating, and when the kits are born, he does not help raise them. The kits nurse on their mother's milk. She must continue to feed herself while she nurses to keep up the energy necessary to produce milk and raise the kits alone.

A mother striped skunk looks after one of her kits.

Did You Know?
Western spotted skunks are true nomads. They rarely make permanent dens, preferring to hole up in hollow logs, in woodpiles, and under rock outcrops.

Chapter Four

A Surfeit of Skunks

Scientists have puzzled over where skunks should be classified in the animal kingdom. For many years, scientists believed that skunks were basically weasels. Today, skunks are in the order Carnivora and have their own separate family called Mephitidae (meh-FIH-tih-dee). Skunks are divided into three different groups and ten species.

Striped and hooded skunks are members of the *Mephitis* **genus.** Both species live in North America. Striped skunks have the widest distribution area, covering most of Canada, all of the United States, and northern Mexico. This species is the largest skunk and has the most recognizable pattern of stripes on its fur. When striped skunks defend themselves, they turn their bodies into a U-shape. With their eyes on their target, they let loose their pungent spray.

Striped skunks prefer living in mixed woods, grasslands, and open prairie. Having a den close to water is ideal, although skunks do not drink large amounts of water. Skunks like living near people and fit right in to city

*Some skunks living near people, like this striped skunk,
raid garbage cans in search of food.*

and suburban homes. Suburban families with skunks nearby may find their front yards pockmarked with small holes where skunks have dug for grubs.

Hooded skunks live in the southwestern United States, in all of Mexico, and south to Costa Rica. This species likes dry scrub, desert, and grassland habitats. Like the striped skunk, the hooded skunk has a thin white stripe on the forehead. However, instead of two stripes on the body, the hooded skunk's entire back and tail are white.

The hooded skunk's tail is truly spectacular and is usually longer than its body. Tails are white and feathery and measure 37 centimeters (14.5 inches). Hooded skunks feed primarily on insects, although they also eat small rodents. A real treat for hooded skunks is the fruit of the prickly pear cactus.

Spotted skunks belong to the genus *Spilogale* and are small and more weasel-like than striped skunks. Their patterns are unusual and even beautiful, but they still pack a stink bomb that sends large bears on the run. Spotted skunks, like other skunk species, emerge from their dens in twilight and hunt through the night. They have excellent hearing and smell, but their vision is poor. Poor vision is fairly common among night predators, as they can use

Raised in the air, this hooded skunk's tail towers over the rest of its body.

The white stripe from the top of its head to its tail is another distinctive feature of the hog-nosed skunk.

their hearing and sense of smell to locate the next victim.

Members of the genus *Conepatus*, hog-nosed skunks get their name from their pig-shaped noses. Because they use their noses to snuffle through the underbrush for food, they are also called "rooter" skunks. Hog-nosed skunks live in southwestern United States, all of Central America, and as far south as Argentina. Hog-nosed skunks are the only skunks found in South America. The bare snout species uses its powerful nose in combination with its strong front feet when hunting such favorite foods as beetles, grubs, and larvae. These skunks prefer to live near rivers, in canyons, and on rocky cliffs. They can dig their own dens but happily take over the empty dens of other animals. These skunks avoid really dense forests and can live at elevations up to 4,100 meters (13,400 feet) in the Andes Mountains.

Some members of the hog-nosed skunk genus seem unaffected by venom from such snakes as the pit viper or rattlesnake. This has led scientists to wonder whether hog-nosed skunks eat venomous snakes. On the other hand, it is possible that the resistance to venom helps the skunks get away from snakes that might want to eat them.

An American badger, a relative of the skunk, climbs out of its den.

A SKUNK'S RELATIVES: THE MUSTELIDAE FAMILY

Skunks were once thought to be part of the Mustelidae (mus-TEL-ih-dee) family, the largest family of carnivores. This family includes weasels, otters, badgers, wolverines, stoats, polecats, martens, minks, and fishers. In all, there are fifty-six species of Mustelidae. Skunks, once listed as mustelids, now have their own family.

North America is home to a wide variety of weasels and their relatives. On the west coast of California and Canada, sea otters float on rolling ocean waves. Inland, river otters slide into the water with an ease and grace that would make Olympic swimmers jealous.

Badgers show a remarkable talent for digging. They hollow out comfortable dens that are sometimes taken over by skunks. Black-footed ferrets share the same habitat as prairie dogs. Because prairie dogs are forever digging new burrows with extra rooms throughout, the ferrets simply locate an empty room and move into it.

Several members of the weasel family have earned reputations as predators. Fishers have developed a system for preying on porcupines. They attack the porcupine's face repeatedly until it is too weak to resist. Then the porcupine is flipped on its back. Fishers move in for the kill on the

Did You Know?
Zorillas in Africa look
like skunks, but they are
actually weasels. Zorillas
are also called polecats.

porcupine's tender belly. Wolverines are the only animals that kill for the sake of killing. Wolverines hunt far more meat than they can possibly eat. They cache the rest in a pantry for eating at a later date.

Are stink badgers skunks or badgers? The answer to that question puzzled scientists. Today, scientists say that they are not skunks. Indonesian stink badgers and Palawan stink badgers, the two species of stink badgers, are squat and stocky with short legs and pointed snouts. Palawan stink badgers tend to be smaller than their Indonesian relatives, and both species have short tails.

Unlike its skunk cousin, the stink badger usually has brown fur with patches of lighter fur on the top of their head. Both caps and stripes range from whitish to yellowish in color and fade away before reaching the animal's back.

Indonesian stink badgers are night hunters, while their Palawan cousins feed day or night. An ideal stink badger menu features insects as an appetizer and earthworms as the main course.

Stink badgers generally dig their own dens, although some have been known to move into porcupine burrows. Occasionally, the porcupines are still living in the burrows at the time. It appears that even a prickly porcupine will not risk trying to oust a stinky roommate.

The first line of defense for a stink badger is to roll over and play dead. This seems a strange defense, since stink badgers, like skunks, can spray foul-smelling fluid from their anal glands.

Members of the Family Mustelidae

These are some of the animals related to the skunk. Like the skunk, many of these species have been hunted for their fur.

African Clawless Otter (*Aonyx capensis*)
American Badger (*Taxidea taxus*)
Burmese Ferret-Badger (*Melogale personata*)
Chinese Ferret-Badger (*Melogale moschata*)
Everett's Ferret-Badger (*Melogale everetti*)
Giant Otter (*Pteronura brasiliensis*)
Hairy-Nosed Otter (*Lutra sumatrana*)
Hog Badger (*Arctonyx collaris*)
Javan Ferret-Badger (*Melogale orientalis*)
Marine Otter (*Lontra felina*)
Neotropical Otter (*Lontra longicaudis*)
North American River Otter (*Lontra canadensis*)
Sea Otter (*Enhydra lutris*)
Smooth-Coated Otter (*Lutrogale perspicillata*)
Southern River Otter (*Lontra provocax*)
Tayra (*Eira barbara*)

Chapter Five

The Past, Present, and Future

Nine million years ago, a species of skunk roamed the area that is today the Mojave Desert's Red Rock Canyon. The skunk had a number of unusual neighbors—rhinos, three-toed horses, giraffelike camels, saber-toothed cats, alligator lizards, and shrews.

The skunk fossils discovered in Red Rock Canyon are the oldest skunk remains found in North America. According to scientists, this skunk was the smallest of all North American skunks, measuring less than 30 centimeters (1 foot) and weighing just a few ounces.

Early skunks evolved into the several species that live in North and South America today. At one time, skunks were far more plentiful than they are now. As is true for many fur-bearing species, trapping and over-hunting reduced skunk populations.

Did You Know?
Skunks cannot see objects located more than 3 meters (9.8 feet) away clearly.

*Humans have made a huge impact on the populations
of spotted skunks and other skunk species.*

*This drawing shows a fashionable woman of the 1920s
wearing a fur coat made from mole and skunk!*

Skunk pelts, particularly striped skunk fur, brought high prices on the fur market. Trappers passed off skunk fur as marten fur until laws required more accurate labeling. While many women did not mind wearing marten, wearing skunk was less appealing.

It is unfortunate that so many skunks were hunted for their fur, since skunks are particularly useful in controlling rodent populations in rural, urban, and suburban areas. Spotted skunks are the best rodent hunters, although other skunk species catch their share of rats and mice.

Although rodent control is important, skunks also are known to carry diseases. Like many wild animals, they can carry ticks, roundworms, and **parasites.** These creatures can be passed to household pets and must be cleared up with the help of a veterinarian.

Of greater concern is rabies. The Centers for Disease Control and Prevention (CDC) monitors several diseases in the United States and around the world. The center recorded more than two thousand cases of rabies in skunks during 2000. Rabies, caused by a virus, is carried in saliva and passed to humans through animal bites. When humans contract rabies, they suffer from fever, depression, muscle spasms, sensitivity to light and noise, and difficulty swallowing. Without treatment, humans infected with rabies die.

The threat of getting rabies from a skunk is small. Since 1995, there has not been a human death caused by a bite from a rabid skunk, according to the CDC. However, that does not mean humans should act foolishly when they see wild skunks. The best plan is to watch the skunk from a distance and avoid any physical contact.

THREATS TO SURVIVAL

Skunks suffer from the same threats as most other wild species. As humans clear land for farms and housing, skunks must find new habitats. Luckily, skunks adapt easily to change. If there is no place to dig a burrow, skunks simply move into a house, barn, or office building. Since skunks like to move around, they will move on within a few days or weeks. If you find one living nearby, do not try to oust the skunk with a pole or pitchfork. That will result in getting a dose of skunk spray. Then, even after the skunk leaves, its memory—or odor—will linger on.

Several species of skunks are considered rare. A combination of overhunting, loss of habitat, increase in predators, and disease has reduced certain skunk populations. Pygmy spotted skunks and eastern spotted skunks are protected by law. In several South

American nations, hog-nosed skunks also enjoy some legal protection.

Few scientists have performed in-depth studies of skunks, and an accurate census of any skunk population does not exist. For that reason, it is difficult to decide whether a skunk species is at risk. The best thing that humans can do for skunks is what apparently works best—leave them alone.

The harvesting of forests for lumber and paper products is also destroying skunk habitats.

Glossary

anus (AY-nuss) the opening on an animal through which solid waste passes out of the body

aposematic (ap-uh-suh-MAT-ik) colored in a way that indicates special abilities for defense

arachnids (uh-RAK-nidz) any wingless animal with a hard exoskeleton, such as spiders, scorpions, mites, and ticks

caches (KA-shez) places where animals collect and store food for later use

carrion (KAYR-ee-un) dead or rotting flesh

delayed implantation (dee-LAYD im-plan-TAY-shun) a process in which a female mates but does not become pregnant with young until much later

embryos (EM-bree-ohz) the developing young of an animal prior to birth or hatching

genus (JEE-nuss) a category of classification made up of related organisms, which can be further divided into species

hibernate (HY-bur-nayt) to spend the winter in a sleeplike state

omnivores (OM-nuh-vorz) animals that eat both plants and animals

parasites (PAR-uh-sytz) organisms that live on or in an organism of another species

predators (PREH-duh-turz) animals that hunt and kill other animals for food

thiols (THY-allz) chemical compounds that contain sulfur

For More Information

Watch It

Really Wild Animals: Amazing North America, VHS (Washington, D.C.: National Geographic Video, 1997)

Wonders of Nature in Our Backyard: Birds, Frogs, Foxes, Dragonflies, and More! DVD (Atlanta, GA: Marshall Fairman Productions, 2002)

Read It

Bishop, Nic. *Forest Explorer: A Life-Sized Field Guide*. New York: Scholastic Press, 2004.

Kalman, Bobbie. *A Forest Habitat*. New York: Crabtree Publishing Company, 2006.

Markle, Sandra. *Skunks*. Minneapolis, MN: Lerner Publications, 2007.

Mason, Adrienne. *Skunks*. Tonawanda, NY: Kids Can Press, 2006.

Nelson, Kristin L. *Spraying Skunks*. Minneapolis, MN: Lerner Publishing, 2003.

Somervill, Barbara A. *Forests*. Chanhassen, MN: The Child's World, 2005.

Souza, D. M. *Skunks Do More Than Stink!* Brookfield, CT: Copper Beech, 2002.

Stone, Tanya. *Wild America: Skunk*. Belmont, CA: Blackbirch Press, 2002.

Whitehouse, Patricia. *Skunks*. Chicago: Heinemann Library, 2002.

Look It Up

Visit our Web page for lots of links about skunks:
http://www.childsworld.com/links

Note to Parents, Teachers, and Librarians: We routinely verify our Web links to make sure they are safe, active sites—so encourage your readers to check them out!

The Animal Kingdom
Where Do Skunks Fit In?

Kingdom: Animalia

Phylum: Chordata (animals with backbones)

Class: Mammalia

Order: Carnivora

Family: Mephitidae

Genus: *Conepatus, Mephitis, Spilogale*

Index

About the Author

Sophie Lockwood is a former teacher and a longtime writer. She writes textbooks, newspaper articles, and magazine articles. Sophie enjoys writing about animals and their habits. The most interesting part of her research, Sophie says, is learning how scientists apply their knowledge to save endangered species. She lives with her husband in the foothills of the Blue Ridge Mountains.

Library of Congress Cataloging-in-Publication Data

Watts, Barrie.
   Mushroom.

   (Stopwatch books)
   Includes index.
   Summary: Discusses the parts of mushrooms and
how these fungi grow.
   I. Mushrooms—Juvenile literature. [I. Mushrooms]
I. Title. II. Series.
QK6l7.W37   1986   589.2'223   86-6659
ISBN 0-382-0930l-l
ISBN 0-382-09287-2 (lib. bdg.)

First published by A & C Black (Publishers) Limited
35 Bedford Row, London WC1R 4JH

© 1986 Barrie Watts

First published in the United States in 1986
by Silver Burdett Company
Morristown, New Jersey

Acknowledgements
The artwork is by Helen Senior.
The publishers would like to thank Jean Imrie for her help and advice.